The Enlightenment

A Revolution in Reason

Patrice Sherman

Publishing Credits

Dona Herweck Rice, *Editor-in-Chief*;
Lee Aucoin, *Creative Director*;
Torrey Maloof, *Editor*;
Neri Garcia, *Senior Designer*;
Stephanie Reid, *Photo Researcher*;
Rachelle Cracchiolo, M.S.Ed., *Publisher*

Image Credits

Teacher Created Materials

5301 Oceanus Drive
Huntington Beach, CA 92649-1030
http://www.tcmpub.com

ISBN 978-1-4333-5013-9

© 2013 Teacher Created Materials, Inc.

Table of Contents

Words That Changed the World

In June 1776, future U.S. president Thomas Jefferson wrote these famous words: "We hold these truths to be self-evident, that all men are created equal." Jefferson did not live in a world of equality. Men who owned land had more power than those who did not. Women had very few rights. Slavery still existed. The **Declaration of Independence**, which Jefferson helped author, did not change those things. Yet Jefferson's words meant something. They presented a **radical** idea. His words were a sign that things were beginning to change.

Jefferson was part of a movement called the **Enlightenment** (en-LAHYT-n-muhnt). Enlightenment **philosophers** sought wisdom. These scholars, or thinkers, used **reason** to solve problems. They believed in religious freedom, individual rights, and self-government.

a gathering of Enlightenment leaders

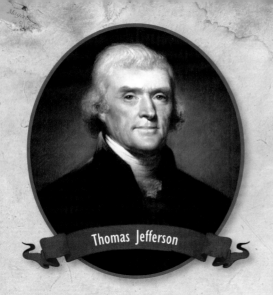

Thomas Jefferson

The Enlightenment not only changed politics, it changed science and art, too. Scientists used reason to conduct experiments. They learned from observation. Artists expressed new ideals of truth and beauty. The Enlightenment transformed Europe and America. It offered hope for human rights and freedom.

To Enlighten

To enlighten means to give knowledge. In 1784, philosopher Immanuel Kant (ih-MAN-yoo-uhl kahnt) wrote an essay on enlightenment. Kant stated that people should not be afraid to think for themselves. Later, historians used the word *enlightenment* to refer to the period of time when people in the Western world developed new approaches to science, government, and education.

Man of the People

Thomas Jefferson was a philosopher, scientist, and politician. He was also the third president of the United States and helped establish the Library of Congress.

Setting the Stage for New Ideas

The Thirty Years' War

From 1618 to 1648, the countries of Europe engaged in a series of conflicts known as the Thirty Years' War. Tension between **Protestants** and **Catholics** helped start the war. Political battles among royal families also played a part.

At the start of the seventeenth century, European nations did not have fixed borders. Most people did not think of themselves as **citizens** of a state. They gave their loyalty to the lord who held power over their area. Fights over land were common and violent. Soldiers, called *mercenaries* (MUR-suh-ner-eez), were paid to fight. Mercenaries were often poor men willing to work for whichever lord promised them the most money.

battle during the Thirty Years' War, Germany, 1631

Over 20 nations took part in the Thirty Years' War. The Protestant nations included England, Scotland, Sweden, and Prussia. The Catholic nations included France and the Holy Roman Empire.

The long war caused a massive shortage of food. This led to widespread hunger. Destruction and disease devastated Central Europe. Soldiers looted villages and burned farms. Thousands of people were driven from their lands. By the 1630s, Europeans, both rich and poor, had become tired of constant conflict.

Martin Luther

The Peace of Westphalia

Between 1643 and 1648, representatives of the nations involved in the war met in Münster, which is in modern-day Germany. There they signed a series of peace treaties, or agreements. The Thirty Years' War was finally over.

Known as the Peace of Westphalia (west-FEY-lee-uh), the treaties did several important things. First, they set clear borders between nations. This created the nation state of modern Europe. The treaties also said that nations now had the right to defend their borders from invasion.

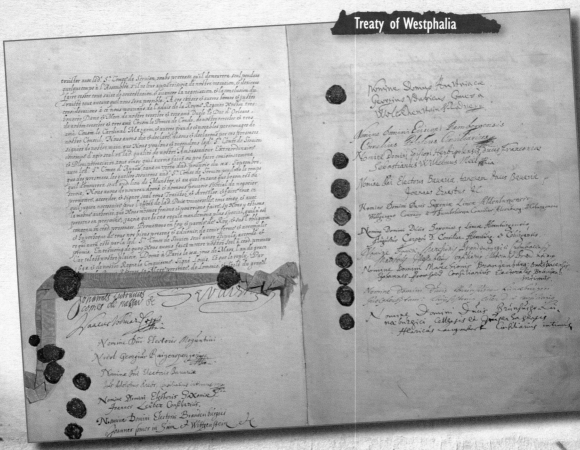

Treaty of Westphalia

signing the treaty of Münster, which became part of the Peace of Westphalia

Religion was also addressed in the treaties. Each ruler would have the right to decide on the official religion of his country. Protestants in Catholic countries and Catholics in Protestant countries would still have the right to observe their own religion as long as they followed certain rules. They might not be allowed to hold public services. Or, they might be limited to meeting only at certain times of the day. This was not complete religious freedom. However, it was a big step toward tolerance, or acceptance.

After the Peace of Westphalia, Europeans began to focus on law, education, and science. This was the beginning of the Enlightenment.

The Natural Lawyer

Born into a wealthy Dutch family, Hugo Grotius (GROH-shee-uhs) studied at the University of Leiden (LAHYD-n) at age 11. He believed that all nations should respect certain laws. He called this *natural law*. His ideas later became the basis for international law.

The Great Educator

John Comenius (kuh-MEE-nee-uhs) was one of the first people to believe that everyone should have access to education. He helped establish schools throughout Europe. His methods included using books with pictures to teach children.

England's Glorious Revolution

During the 1660s, England began to experience increasing tension between the king and **Parliament** (PAHR-luh-muhnt). In 1685, James II, a Catholic, took the throne. England was a Protestant nation. People feared that James would try to force his faith on them. James's behavior did not help matters. He believed that the king should have absolute power. When Parliament objected to his actions, James tried to get rid of Parliament.

In 1688, James II was overthrown and replaced by King William and Queen Mary. The new rulers agreed to a written **constitution**. The constitution limited the power of the king and increased the power of Parliament.

William and Mary become king and queen.

In 1689, Parliament passed England's first Bill of Rights. Under this bill, the king could not get rid of Parliament. Individuals had the right to **petition** the government. **Cruel and unusual punishment** was also forbidden.

In addition, the Bill of Rights supported the Habeas Corpus (HEY-bee-uhs KAWR-puhs) Act of 1679. This act stated that anyone arrested must be charged with a crime. If they were not charged, then they had to be released. This meant that people could not be arrested simply for expressing their political or religious beliefs.

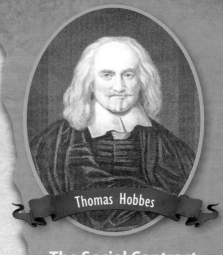

Thomas Hobbes

The Social Contract

Thomas Hobbes (hobz) was the first philosopher to introduce the **social contract** theory. He believed that kings could only rule with the consent of their subjects. Though he did not live to see the Glorious Revolution, his ideas provided the foundation for the Bill of Rights.

Parliament

Parliament is England's ruling body. It includes the House of Lords and the House of Commons. Members of the House of Lords are **aristocrats** who inherit their seats in Parliament. Members of the House of Commons are **commoners** elected by the people.

Philosophy: An Age of Ideas

After the Thirty Years' War ended, people throughout Europe began to think about the kind of society they wanted. What kinds of laws were best? How could people use reason to understand the world around them? Philosophical questions were not just for scholars. They were for everyone.

John Locke

In England, John Locke (lok) became one of the leading philosophers of the Enlightenment. Locke studied medicine at Oxford (OKS-ferd) University. After he graduated, he worked as a doctor.

John Locke

Locke thought deeply about how people acquired knowledge. In 1689, he wrote *An Essay Concerning Human Understanding*. Locke argued that humans were not born with knowledge. He said that they gain it through education. Locke believed the mind at birth was like a blank slate, or *tabula rasa* (TAB-yuh-luh RAH-suh). Reason was the most important function of the mind. All people, Locke declared, could learn to use reason.

Locke also promoted the ideas of the social contract and the separation of church and state. Locke's theories were daring and new. His influence stretched far beyond England to France and America.

Oxford University in the seventeenth century

Empiricism

Empiricism (em-PIR-uh-siz-uhm) is a branch of philosophy that emphasizes direct experience. Empiricists believe that humans learn about the world mainly through their physical senses—sight, sound, touch, taste, and smell. Empirical evidence is evidence that can be observed and measured. A scientific experiment is one way of obtaining empirical evidence.

Classical Liberalism

During the Enlightenment, liberalism was defined as a belief in limited government and the rule of law. Liberals supported individual liberties such as freedom of speech and religion. Though the definition of liberalism has changed over time, Locke is still considered the father of classic liberalism.

David Hume

Like Locke, the Scottish philosopher David Hume (hyoom) believed in the use of observation and experience to gain knowledge. But unlike Locke, Hume believed emotions were as important as intelligence. Human nature was a mixture of the two. Without emotion, humans would have no motivation. They would have no drive to achieve anything.

Hume did not mean that people could just give in to their passions without thinking. Rather, Hume believed that people were capable of free will. They could decide between right and wrong. Hume promoted skepticism (SKEP-tuh-siz-uhm). Skepticism is the idea that people should be critical of any theory until it is proven.

David Hume

A
TREATISE
OF
Human Nature:

BEING

An ATTEMPT to introduce the ex-
perimental Method of Reasoning

INTO

MORAL SUBJECTS.

by David Hume Esqr.

Rara temporum felicitas, ubi sentire, quæ velis; & quæ
sentias, dicere licet.   TACIT.

BOOK I.

OF THE

UNDERSTANDING.

LONDON:
Printed for JOHN NOON, at the White-Hart, near
Mercer's-Chapel in Cheapside.
MDCCXXXIX.

title page to Hume's *A Treatise* of *Human Nature*

Skepticism

To be skeptical means to have doubts. A skeptic does not accept anything on blind faith. Skeptics need to see proof. In Hume's day, many skeptics believed that nothing could ever be proven to be completely true. There would always be room for doubt. There would always be questions without answers.

The Science of Man

Hume applied Isaac Newton's scientific method to his study of human nature. Just as scientists only know what they can observe, people can only know what they experience. Hume said there is no knowledge outside of experience.

Hume wrote on a wide variety of subjects. His favorite was human nature. He wanted to know how experience shaped thoughts and emotions. Hume often used the phrase "the science of man" to describe his work. Many historians consider Hume to be one of the first psychologists (sahy-KOL-uh-jists). Psychologists study the science behind the human mind and behavior.

Voltaire

François-Marie Arouet (FRAN-swah ma-REE AH-roo-ay) was born in a French province in 1694. He wanted to be one thing when he grew up—a writer. By his late teens, he was living in Paris writing poetry. Many of Arouet's poems poked fun at the government. In 1717, a judge sentenced him to prison because of it.

When Arouet was released a year later, he continued to criticize authority. In 1718, Arouet changed his name to Voltaire (vohl-TAIR). Voltaire is a made-up word. It suggested something swift and bright, like a bolt of lightening.

No subject was **taboo** for Voltaire. He disliked organized religion. He called himself a *deist* (DEE-ist). A deist is a person who believes in a god but does not belong to a religion. Voltaire fought against laws that could imprison people without trial. He was also against slavery and **intolerance** of any kind.

Voltaire in prison

Voltaire is arrested again in Prussia.

Candide

In 1759, Voltaire wrote *Candide* (kahn-DEED). The main character, Candide, is a young man who believes everything happens for the best. But in the end, Candide decides that people must make their own happiness.

Satire

Satire (SAT-ahyir) is a form of writing that uses humor to criticize people and ideas. Irony is often used in satires. Irony is a statement that says one thing but means its opposite. Voltaire's use of irony and satire in *Candide* made it one of the most popular books written during the Enlightenment.

Voltaire had to flee France quite often to avoid arrest, but he never stopped writing. People in France loved to hear him speak and read his works. For many French citizens, Voltaire became the voice of the Enlightenment. He was a philosopher dedicated to the freedom of the individual to think and speak as he or she pleased.

The Scientific Revolution

The scientific revolution began in the sixteenth century. It was then that Copernicus (koh-PUR-ni-kuhs) discovered that Earth moved around the sun. This discovery made people look at the universe with new eyes. Observations, measurements, and experiments became the traits of science. People saw that the natural world had laws that could be explained by scientific methods. Over the next century, **astronomy**, physics, mathematics, chemistry, and medicine were transformed by this new approach to learning.

Johannes Kepler

At the age of six, Johannes (yoh-HAN-es) Kepler saw the Great Comet of 1577. It soared across the night sky. At that moment, he fell in love with astronomy. **Smallpox** had weakened Kepler's eyes, but that did not stop him. Kepler had trouble seeing the heavens, but he could still use the observations of others to make measurements.

Kepler's model shows the elliptical orbits of planets.

Copernicus

Before Copernicus, astronomers believed all heavenly bodies revolved around Earth. But if this were true, Copernicus wondered, why did planets sometimes appear to move backward? Why were their orbits different sizes? His research convinced him that Earth revolved around the sun, and modern science was born.

Supernova

On October 9, 1604, a star appeared in the sky that was so bright it could be seen during the day. In 1606, Kepler published an essay on his observations. The star became known as SN 1604, or Kepler's Supernova. In the twenty-first century, it still remains visible at night.

In the early 1600s, Kepler published his laws of planetary motion. These laws said that all planets moved around the sun. They moved in elliptical, or oval, orbits. Kepler stated that these orbits, or paths, all had the same mathematical properties. It did not matter how large or small their orbits were. Kepler's work later helped Isaac Newton develop his laws of motion and gravity.

Johannes Kepler

Galileo

Like Copernicus and Kepler, Galileo Galilei (gal-uh-LEY-oh gal-lee-LEY) knew that the planets revolved around the sun. This meant that the solar system was heliocentric (hee-lee-oh-SEN-trik).

Galileo started his career as a mathematician. He taught in Italian universities. There are many stories about how he dropped cannonballs of different weights from the Tower of Pisa. He was trying to prove that all objects fall at the same rate.

In 1609, Galileo built the most powerful telescope of his time. The telescope could enlarge objects up to 20 times their actual size. A year later, he became the first person to observe the moons of Jupiter. He was the first to describe the rings of Saturn, the surface of the moon, sunspots, and the individual stars of the Milky Way.

Galileo drops objects from the Tower of Pisa.

Galileo's discoveries threatened the powerful Roman Catholic Church. The Church said that the solar system was not heliocentric. That kind of thinking went against the teachings of the Bible. The Church forced Galileo to recant, or take back, his theories. He was placed under house arrest for the rest of his life. Nothing, however, could destroy his impact on science.

Francis Bacon

Francis Bacon helped develop the scientific method. He called for the use of **inductive reasoning** to solve problems. *Inductive* means drawing general conclusions from specific observations. When scientists measure the results of experiments to prove or disprove a theory, they are using inductive reasoning.

Van Leeuwenhoek

While other scientists were busy studying the heavens, Antonie van Leeuwenhoek (AN-toh-nee van LEY-vuhn-hook) discovered a universe in a drop of water. He built his own **microscopes**. In the 1670s, he became the first to observe tiny organisms he called *animalcules* (an-uh-MAL-kyools). His work led to the development of modern **microbiology**.

the trial of Galileo

It seemed unlikely that Isaac Newton would become a scientist. When he was 17, Newton's mother put him in charge of the family farm. Newton had little interest in farming, but his father had died and he had to take charge. However, Newton still spent most of his time reading in the village bookshop. The local schoolmaster noticed Newton's love of reading. He told Newton's mother to send Newton back to school. Newton grew up to become one of the greatest scientists in history.

Isaac Newton

Newton believed the simplest explanation was often the best. He changed the study of **physics**. He defined the basic laws of motion. His universal law of gravity and three laws of motion proved that Earth did revolve around the sun.

Descartes

René Descartes (dey-KAHRT) combined the study of philosophy, mathematics, and science. He helped develop modern algebra, geometry, anatomy, and optics, or the study of light. His research on the human brain focused on the pineal (PIN-ee-uhl) gland. This small gland makes a substance related to waking and sleeping.

Pascal

In 1642, 19-year-old Blaise Pascal (bleyz pah-SKAHL) invented a machine to help his father calculate taxes. It was called the Pascaline. It was the world's first mechanical calculator. Pascal went on to become a philosopher, scientist, and mathematician. In 1971, one of the first computer programming languages was named after him.

Newton also studied the color **spectrum** of light. He developed new methods of calculus, too. His book, *Mathematical Principles of Natural Philosophy*, made Newton famous in Europe. Newton remained modest. He knew he owed much to earlier scientists. "If I have seen further," he wrote to a friend, "it is by standing on the shoulders of giants."

Newton studies the color spectrum of light.

Romanticism, Reason, and Rousseau

Not everybody was convinced that reason was the path to truth. Not all truth was scientific, they argued. Art, music, and literature revealed another kind of truth. This truth could only be reached through emotion. This idea became known as **Romanticism** (roh-MAN-tuh-siz-uhm). Romantics believed nature was not an object to be studied. Nature was a source of deep wonder and delight.

Jean-Jacques Rousseau

From his earliest days, Jean-Jacques Rousseau (zhahn zhahk roo-SOH) loved to read. Often, he would stay up all night reading adventure stories. Later, he would consider childhood to be the most important stage of life. This was a completely new idea. For most of European history, children had been treated as small adults. Rousseau believed children should be taught to use reason, but he also respected their young emotions. He thought children should learn through their own experiences.

Rousseau thought humans were naturally good. This was a radical idea. The closer they remained to nature, the better humans would be. If given the chance, Rousseau believed that people would naturally choose the best form of government. His volume, *The Social Contract*, became one of the most important books of the Enlightenment.

Robinson Crusoe

Diderot's Encyclopedia

Philosopher Denis Diderot (duh-NEE DEE-duh-roh) believed that art was as important to education as writing. He wanted everybody to have access to knowledge. Diderot edited the first major French encyclopedia of art and science. It was published between 1751 and 1772. All 28 volumes were illustrated with drawings and diagrams.

Robinson Crusoe

One of the books Rousseau suggested children should read was *Robinson Crusoe*. Written by Daniel Defoe (dih-FOH), *Robinson Crusoe* tells the story of a shipwrecked sailor who learns to survive on a tropical island with the help of a native man he calls Friday. Rousseau believed the novel encouraged self-reliance.

Benjamin Franklin

Benjamin Franklin was an American philosopher. He founded the first post office and volunteer fire department in Philadelphia. He worked as a printer, a postmaster, a politician, a scientist, an inventor, and a diplomat. His *Poor Richard's Almanack* gave advice in short, witty statements called *aphorisms* (AF-uh-riz-uhmz)—a form of philosophy everyone could enjoy!

The Iroquois Confederacy

The U.S. founding fathers did not get all their ideas from Europe. Many historians believe that they were also influenced by the Iroquois (IR-uh-kwoi) **Confederacy.** This was a group of five American Indian tribes that had banded together for mutual support. The Confederacy met every year to settle disputes between tribes.

An Age of Revolutions

The Enlightenment was not just an age of ideas; it was an age of action as well. In the late eighteenth century, two revolutions rocked the Western world. The first, in America, succeeded. The second, in France, failed in many ways. Both revolutions left a legacy of change. After the Enlightenment, democracy was not just a theory, but a reality.

the American Revolution

The American Revolution

The British government ruled the American colonists without their consent. Because of this, the colonists said they had the right to create their own government. The colonists wanted a nation ruled by laws, not kings. When the Declaration of Independence was written in 1776, the colonists were guided by John Locke's theory of the social contract.

After six years of war, the British surrendered in 1781. Colonial leaders wrote the Constitution of the United States. It said that all citizens would enjoy freedom of religion and speech, among other rights. It stated that the government would be divided into three branches—executive, legislative (LEJ-is-ley-tiv), and judicial (joo-DISH-uhl). This created a balance of powers. No one branch could control the others. By 1791, the Constitution had been ratified, or approved. A new era had begun.

The French Revolution

France in the eighteenth century was a nation of extreme contrasts. It was home to some of the greatest thinkers of the Enlightenment. It was also ruled by a king with absolute power. It was a country known for art, music, and literature. Yet most people lived in ignorance and poverty.

Inspired by the American Revolution in the summer of 1789, angry French subjects stormed the Bastille (ba-STEEL), a prison in France. They then marched on to the king's palace in Versailles (ver-SAHY). They demanded justice. In August, they signed the Declaration of the Rights of Man and of the Citizen. It stated that all citizens were equal and born with natural rights. It called for the freedom of press, speech, and religion.

The French Revolution then dissolved into fighting and violence. Thousands were executed, including the king and his family. War broke out between France and its neighbors. In 1799, Napoleon Bonaparte (nuh-POH-lee-uhn BOH-nuh-pahrt) seized power and declared himself emperor in 1804.

The Revolution was over. It was not a complete failure, however. The French had changed history. They had gone from being subjects to citizens. Europe would never be the same, and the great thinkers of the Enlightenment ensured that the world would never be the same.

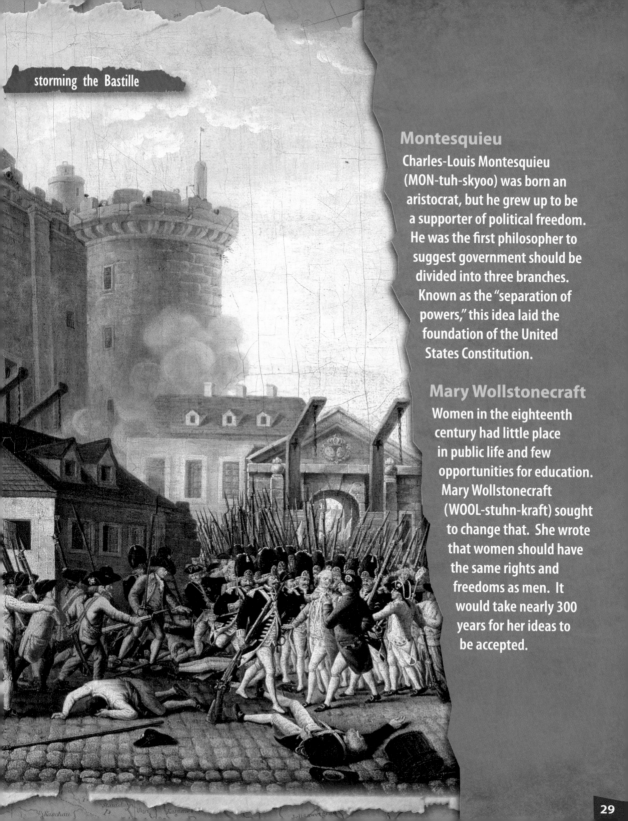

storming the Bastille

Montesquieu

Charles-Louis Montesquieu (MON-tuh-skyoo) was born an aristocrat, but he grew up to be a supporter of political freedom. He was the first philosopher to suggest government should be divided into three branches. Known as the "separation of powers," this idea laid the foundation of the United States Constitution.

Mary Wollstonecraft

Women in the eighteenth century had little place in public life and few opportunities for education. Mary Wollstonecraft (WOOL-stuhn-kraft) sought to change that. She wrote that women should have the same rights and freedoms as men. It would take nearly 300 years for her ideas to be accepted.

Glossary

aphorisms—short sentences that contain general truths

aristocrats—members of an upper class that usually hold power

astronomy—the science of the heavenly bodies

Catholics—members of the Roman Catholic Church

citizens—legally recognized members of a nation or state

commoners—people with little money or power

confederacy—an alliance of states or organizations

constitution—a document giving the principles on which a state is organized

cruel and unusual punishment—discipline that is more severe than the crime that was committed

Declaration of Independence—a document stating that the colonies in America were breaking away from Great Britain

Enlightenment—the period of European and American history from roughly 1630 to 1800, which witnessed the development of the scientific revolutions and the growth of democratic ideals

inductive reasoning—a method of establishing a general principle through the observation of individual examples

intolerance—treating unfairly for no legitimate reason

microbiology—a branch of biology that focuses on microscopic life

microscopes—instruments that use lenses to make small objects appear larger

Parliament—a governing body in the United Kingdom

petition—to make a formal request

philosophers—people who study human thought

physics—a science that deals with matter and energy

Protestant Reformation—a split in Western Christianity in the sixteenth century that resulted in the creation of Protestant Churches in opposition to the Roman Catholic Church

Protestants—people who protested against the Roman Catholic Church

radical—different from the established ideas and social structures

reason—the things that make facts understandable

Romanticism—the idea that humans experience life mainly through their emotions, not their intellect

smallpox—a disease that was often deadly and left scars on the victims

social contract—an agreement between members of society, or the idea that government should be based on the consent of the governed

spectrum—the group of colors coming from white light

taboo—not socially normal

Index

Your Turn!

The British government ruled the American colonies without their consent. The colonists said they had the right to create their own government. They wanted a nation ruled by laws, not kings. The colonists looked to John Locke's theory of the social contract when they wrote the Declaration of Independence in 1776.

Rally the Troops

Imagine that you are the leader of the colonial militia in this painting. It is your job to rally the troops before battle. Use John Locke's theories to write a motivational speech that will get the men pumped up to win the fight.